Bethany Clark

I love
horses

HORSES

A BOOK OF CHILDREN'S STORIES

PHOTOGRAPHS BY YANN ARTHUS-BERTRAND
STORIES BY CHRISTOPHE DONNER

Thames & Hudson

Contents

With Hooves in the Air ★ 5

The Other Side of the Storm ★ 8

The Dream Race ★ 11

The Truth about Fish ★ 15

My Kingdom for a Horse ★ 21

My Uncles in America ★ 26

A Desert Rescue ★ 32

The Most Beautiful Horse in the World ★ 34

The Three Tenors ★ 41

Augustine's Obsession ★ 47

Three Little Words ★ 50

The Curse of Devil's Mountain ★ 54

With Hooves in the Air

Gaspard was fed up with watching planes in the sky. He lived alone in his meadow, and the only entertainment he had all day long was watching the planes, which always flew past at exactly the same time. One fine day, when he was watching the Tokyo to Bogota jumbo jet, Gaspard fell flat on his back. And there he lay, with hooves in the air, and not the slightest desire to get up again.

'Maybe I'm dead,' he said to himself. 'Perhaps the years fly by as quickly as the planes, and now my hour has come.'

'Get up, Gascard! You can't just lie there,' said Gilbert, his owner. 'It looks bad.'

As he didn't move, Gilbert tried to entice him with some fresh carrots. 'Come on, then! Come and taste these lovely fresh carrots.'

Not a twitch. And sugar and artichokes had exactly the same effect.

'For heaven's sake! Get up, now! If only you could see yourself!' But it was no use. He was as stubborn as a mule.

Gilbert went to fetch an old friend of Gaspard's. 'You remember Grizelda, don't you? The grey mare?' But Gaspard pretended he didn't know her.

Gilbert decided to ring Mr Paul, the vet. As it happened, Mr Paul had a few cows to look at in the neighbourhood, so he came almost at once, in his suede boots and woolly hat, hand-knitted by his mum. Mr Paul wasn't like other vets – he didn't believe in medicines and never prescribed them.

'I see,' he said, climbing onto Gaspard's belly in order to have a good look at him. 'This horse is perfectly fine. He hasn't even got a temperature.'

'So what's the matter with him?'

'Laziness,' said Mr Paul.

Word got around, and people started to panic. The schoolmistress arrived with a bucket of cold water, which she threw over Gaspard's head. That was what she did to naughty children at school, but it didn't make them any less naughty, and it didn't make Gaspard any less lazy.

Hearing the news from his secretary, the Lord Mayor arrived as well. He wasn't happy.

'What's this all about? Come on, get up, you lazy good-for-nothing! Just what do you think you're up to? The tourist season is about to begin, everyone's ready, the museum, the four-star hotel, Mrs Mitchell's restaurant, the castle all lit up – everything! It's not as if we're asking a great deal of you. Just to stand up on your own four paws.'

'They're not paws,' said Mr Paul. 'They're hooves.'

'Who cares?' cried the mayor. 'Get this idiot of a horse to stand up – now! The first busload of tourists is due in exactly an hour.'

Mr Paul got to work. He pulled and he pushed, and he twisted and he twiddled. Gaspard let him do whatever he wanted. Only he didn't budge.

'I've got some pep pills,' said the pharmacist. 'Maybe we should give him some.' For years now, her chemist's shop had been full of medicines she hadn't been able to sell. This was her chance. But everybody said no, because they all trusted Mr Paul,

who was now working like mad to try and move Gaspard's body.

'Hey up!' they all shouted encouragingly. 'Hey up!'

The woolly cap his mum had knitted kept falling off Mr Paul's head, and he was beginning to get sick of this whole business.

The busload of tourists arrived. They couldn't tear themselves away, the Japanese, the Texans, the Colombians. They started taking photos and filming this peculiar scene. They even called their friends and sent them photos over the phone.

Gaspard was delighted – nobody had ever paid so much attention to him. In any case, Mr Paul's pushing and pulling made him feel good, and so he was thoroughly happy in every way. All he'd needed was someone to show interest in him and to touch him.

When the Chinese, Slavs and Canadians began to applaud him, Gaspard stood up in order to take a bow, but he rose so suddenly that it was Mr Paul who now found himself flat on his back. Everyone laughed – everyone, that is, except Mr Paul.

The Other Side
of the Storm

★

Since the great storm that had ravaged the whole mountain, all the people had gone. Those who were not dead had run away. The only one that remained was Pablo, together with Hembra, his mare and his sole companion.

To feed him, she had given him her milk. The milk of a mare is the best you can possibly have, and it's even given to sick people. Watching her eat grass, little Pablo had also learned to eat it. With milk and grass, you don't need any other food to help you grow. Though you do need a bit of warmth as well. Hembra slept on her side, and the little boy snuggled up between her legs, covered himself in his red blanket, and he slept like a log. Hembra also found water, because horses need to drink. It was a waterfall in the forest, and they went every morning. With her head, Hembra playfully pushed Pablo into the water.

Pablo and Hembra led a simple life, wandering around, looking for food and for places to sleep. They always found a cave for themselves. Then the next day they would set off again, refreshed and ready for new adventures. They would race rabbits and birds, and even if they had no chance of winning, they still enjoyed themselves.

Sometimes, in the course of their games, they would come upon a particular landscape, and then Pablo would remember. The plain stretched out as far as the eye could see. But there was nothing, nothing, nothing. Stones, stunted trees, sand and wind. The wind sounded like one long and terrible moan. Pablo did not know why he stood there looking endlessly at this sad scene. He did not know why his heart felt tight. He just stood there looking, until his eyes brimmed over with tears. Who was he weeping for, and what was he remembering? There was just time to ask these questions, but then the mood passed, the mysterious sorrow disappeared, and he set off again with Hembra through the forests and the clearings, in search of new games and new places in which to shelter

Pablo was king of the mountain. He had mastered it, and he could cross it in the blink of an eye, without ever feeling tired. When he wanted to go right, Hembra went right. He did not even have to pull the reins – he just had to think 'right', 'left', 'faster', and Hembra would understand and do as he thought. Pablo liked speed, and every day he would get his mare to run faster and faster.

One day, having been carried away by their speed and having for the first time managed to jump across the great precipice, they found themselves high up on the mountain, on top of a great rock from which one could see far and wide. They could see further than Pablo had ever seen before. And so he stayed there, eyes fixed on the horizon, looking to see something, to learn something. That day he managed not to cry. He pressed his legs against Hembra's flanks, made himself tough, and stopped the tears from blurring the view. And then he saw something. A sort of glow. Far, far away.

'We've got to go there,' he thought. Straight away, as if she'd heard his thoughts, Hembra galloped off towards the plain. Nothing could have stopped her. Pablo was shaken like a rag doll, but he clung on to her mane as she carried him away at lightning speed.

Now they were on the plain – the dry, scorched plain, swept by the desolate wind, where they had never yet dared to venture. No one knows how long this extraordinary ride lasted. Hours, maybe even days. But at last they arrived, exhausted, parched, their backs covered with dust, like two ghosts. They had reached the gates of the town.

The survivors of the great storm had been living there for a few years. They recognized the mare by her dappled grey coat, and the child by his red blanket.

Pablo soon learned to speak, write, read, and eat with a knife and fork, and all in record time. He even made several friends. But he was never quite like the other boys. He always had Hembra by his side.

Years passed, the children grew up, and some of them travelled to distant lands, but they never forgot Pablo and Hembra, the inseparable partners whose love had brought them from the other side of the storm.

The Dream Race

It was the month of August in the year of the K. Before that, it had been the year of the J, and the following year would be the year of the L. You may think it's difficult to think up names for horses beginning with K, but it's not hard at all.

This was the very first time I'd set foot on a racecourse. Well, people talk about 'beginner's luck'.

Ready, steady, go!

Karaoke went straight into the lead, followed by *Kangaroo* and *King Kong*. As they passed in front of the stand, *Karaoke* was still ahead, on the inside lane, but *Kondiment* and *Ketchup* were beginning to catch up, along with *Kwestion Mark*, the horse I'd bet all my savings on.

The two favourites, *Kreepy* and *Krawly* had got off to a slow start. As they began the downhill descent, *Kidnapper* came up level with *Karaoke*, and the two colts were neck and neck all the way down until *Kidnapper* suddenly started to gallop and was immediately disqualified, because in these races you're only allowed to trot. *Kimono* (son of last year's winner, *Japanese Jumper*) was now fourth, just behind my *Kwestion Mark*. Two more horses were disqualified – *Kut-Off* and *Kastaway* – but nobody cared because they were both outsiders.

Back on level ground, *Karaoke* – now really on song – was out on his own, several lengths in the lead. But as they approached the hill, *Knitting Needle* began to thread her way through the field, closely followed by *Karrots* and *Kokonuts*, and these four were bunched together as they went up past the wood. Running just behind them was *Kwestion Mark*. My *Kwestion Mark*, on whom my fortune now depended.

At that moment, *Kamikaze* put in an incredible spurt and raced past them all. A gasp of astonishment went up from the stands. Most people were now in despair at the slow progress of *Kreepy* and *Krawly*, who were still lagging in the rear. Then it was announced that two more horses, *Kannoninto* and *Krashinto* had been disqualified because their sulkies had collided.

At the bend, *Kwestion Mark* got trapped on the inside, and I was really worried. There seemed no way out. Halfway round it, the driver tried to force his way off the rails, but it was no good – no-one would let him out.

Then *Karaoke*, who had led from the start, began to fade. *Kamikaze*, setting a suicidal pace, was out in front, and people in the stands were booing. But suddenly, *Kwestion Mark* moved sweetly between *Karrots* and *Kokonuts*, who had no answer to his challenge.

Just 100 metres from the finish, it was between *Kamikaze* and *Kwestion Mark*, and I was shouting my head off. It was a magnificent race, but *Kwestion Mark* did everything that was asked of him, and with a final dash, he got his nose in front and crossed the line first. He trotted on for a while, before coming to a full stop in front of the stands to receive the cheers of the crowd. He had beaten all commas, and he had also made me very, very rich.

The Truth about Fish

Once again I'd forgotten the cheque for my dinner money. It was a bad habit of mine, and I don't know why I did it. On the 15th of every month we had to take our dinner money to school, and every time I forgot.

'What's wrong, Markus?' my mother asked. 'Aren't the school meals any good?'

There was fish, and I like fish. And there were potatoes, and I like potatoes. And there was yoghurt, and apricots, and things like that, and I ate them all up and you certainly couldn't say they were no good. No, that wasn't the reason why I kept forgetting to take the cheque. I just don't know why I forgot.

'Try and remember not to forget,' said Dad. He thought that was very witty, but I didn't find it funny at all.

That morning, before I'd left for school, Mum had asked if I'd remembered to take the cheque. She'd signed it the day before: 8,575 Icelandic crowns, and she'd put it in an envelope.

'Stick it in your bag straight away,' she said.

I said OK, I'll do that. Then I went into my room, and I must have put the cheque on my desk next to my schoolbag, but then I don't know what happened. I was sure I'd put the envelope in my bag, but when I was standing in the bursar's office at midday, I couldn't find the envelope or the cheque anywhere. I went through all my exercise books, all my schoolbooks, all my pockets, turned my bag upside down, emptied it all out. Nothing.

'Markus Jakobson! You've forgotten your dinner money again. This is getting beyond a joke. Wait here. I'm going to have a word with the headmaster.'

All the children went into the dining-room, and I was left standing outside the bursar's office. I was starving. I could smell the fish. Smoked, steamed, grilled, marinated – we eat a lot of fish in Iceland. There's even an African recipe now, with the fish boiled in banana leaves. And a Mexican one, with chocolate sauce. It all helps to cover up the soft texture and the same old taste of cod.

That day it was an Italian recipe, with garlic and tomatoes. My mouth was watering.

No sign of the bursar.

At the same time, back home Mum was hoovering. Thanks to the dog and its hairs, she hoovers every day, because otherwise everywhere gets covered. She went into my room, pushing the door open with the hoover, and there, stuck between my desk and my bed, she found the envelope containing my dinner money.

'Again!' she cried, picking up the envelope. 'What's the matter with that boy?'

She looked at her watch, which said five past twelve, and before you could say 'dinner money', she'd turned off the hoover, put on her black sweater and riding boots, and – without even running the comb through her hair – jumped up on Njall, our pony, and was racing off to the school, which is about five kilometres away.

There are no real horses in Iceland – perhaps because they don't like fish – but we do have big ponies. They don't gallop and they don't trot, but they've got a special way of moving which we call a 'tölt', and it's very smooth and comfortable.

My mother came 'tölting' into the playground.

By the time my mother reached the school, I was in tears. The headmaster himself had come from his office to give me a telling-off.

'Jakobson,' he said, 'you clearly need your head examined.'

'I'll bring you the cheque tomorrow,' I said. 'I promise.'

'I know you'll bring it tomorrow, Jakobson. You always bring it tomorrow! You take an evil delight in making a complete mess of all our accounts, because every single cheque…ugh, but you're incapable of understanding all that! You couldn't care less!'

'And don't try to get round us with your crocodile tears,' added the bursar. 'You are going to stand there until all your friends have finished eating that delicious Sicilian recipe with tomatoes and garlic, cooked entirely in olive oil.'

'And I hope that will teach you a lesson!' said the headmaster.

He was just about to go back to his office when Mum arrived, and dismounted from the handsome Njall, who is world famous because of his fabulous mane.

'Headmaster!' she cried. 'Wait! I have the cheque.'

The headmaster and the bursar turned to butter at the sight of my mother. Everyone turns to butter when they see Mum because she is gorgeous.

'I'm so sorry, gentlemen,' she said. 'I don't know why Markus keeps forgetting the cheque.'

'Well, it really is a bit of a mystery,' said the head-master. 'But all right, since you're here now, dear Grethe, give me the cheque and we'll forget and forgive, but this is the last time.'

And then the most extraordinary thing happened. Something I'd never have dared hope for, but which filled me with joy and gratitude: Mum put her hand in her right pocket, then in her left pocket...and nowhere could she find the envelope with the dinner money.

'I'm sure I took it,' she mumbled, going through her pockets yet again.

But she hadn't got it. The headmaster turned to the bursar, and they both exchanged angry looks. Something had, as people say, got up their noses, and they began to splutter, almost as if they were being strangled:

'That's it! This is intolerable! You're trying to make fools of us!'

Mum looked at them – two angry, red-faced men – and then she looked at me, with my tear stains on my cheeks. And she smelt the fragrance coming from the dining room, the glorious scent of fish cooked the Sicilian way. And in the gentlest of voices, she said:

'Ah, that's what you think, is it? Right, gentlemen, that's it. Markus will never eat in your dining room again.'

She took my hand, we walked across the school playground, and hey up, she helped me onto Njall's back, climbed up behind me, and away we went, happily tölting all the way home. It was the happiest day of my life.

'I've bought some meat,' she said, 'and we'll share it. A nice, juicy steak. It's true, you know – even with fish you can have too much of a good thing…'

My Kingdom for a Horse

✹

The Princess of Coursac, an elderly and eccentric lady from Geneva, had just one passion in life: her white horse Anatole.

Anatole was a Barbary horse. She had seen him born, she had raised him, and she couldn't manage without him. He went with her to all four corners of the Earth – in fact, to wherever her diamond business took her.

Transporting a horse the size of Anatole by plane was no small matter. The princess had had a special cabin built for him, which fitted into the hold of the aircraft – a huge, air-conditioned cabin, that was well padded in case of turbulence. She herself supervised the loading, and she was frequently to be heard shouting at the handlers for being too rough. She also went to see the pilot, the managing director of the airline, and to put it bluntly, she and her horse got on everybody's nerves.

On this particular day, when she arrived at the airport in Bombay, the customs officers, who knew her well, found her particularly edgy.

'Are you sure the weather forecast is good?'

'Excellent, Your Highness, you couldn't have better weather.'

'And what about security? There's no risk of the plane being hijacked, is there?'

'You know, Your Highness, that if there is one thing sacred to all men, even international criminals, it is a horse.'

They watched the Princess of Coursac enter Anatole's cabin, and ten minutes later she came out again, with tears in her eyes. It was touching to see how deeply the old lady loved her horse.

The flight went smoothly enough. When they arrived at Dakar in Senegal, and the princess had driven everyone crazy with her vast amount of valuable luggage, the plane was surrounded by a swarm of customs officers, baggage handlers and hauliers, whose sole task it was to deal with Anatole's cabin. This had been lifted out of the aircraft very carefully, and the chief customs officer conscientiously – though

The old lady went red with rage

was having a meeting with the Secretary General of the United Nations. Within a few minutes, the entire planet had heard about it.

The princess would certainly blame the airline, the Ministry of Transport, and every other authority concerned, and it would become an international scandal. She was, after all, not only immensely rich but also extremely influential in the diplomatic world. There was no telling just where her grief and despair over her dead horse might lead. No one dared to mention the word 'war', but it was on everyone's mind. 'My kingdom for a horse!' a famous king had once cried, and the Princess of Coursac was certainly capable of demanding a kingdom for her horse. So what was to be done?

perhaps also with some sort of premonition – decided to go into the cabin and check that the princess's beloved horse really was inside. He also wanted to see this famous animal for himself. Anyway, in he went.

The white horse was lying on its straw, absolutely still. It took only a few seconds for the chief customs officer to realize that the animal was dead.

Dead. The Princess of Coursac's horse was dead! There was turmoil at the airport, the embassy, the Ministry for Foreign Affairs, and when the news reached the Prime Minister, he telephoned the President, and the President telephoned the President of the Indian Republic, who at that precise moment

The princess got off the plane, and at once she began to look round for Anatole's cabin.

'It's gone, Your Highness,' they told her.

'What do you mean, gone?' she asked.

'Gone. It's on its way to your palace. Everything is fine.'

'You should have waited for me.'

'I'm sorry, Your Highness, we thought you would be pleased.'

The answer was to find another horse to put in the cabin in Anatole's place. A white Barbary, absolutely identical. The Red Guard were mobilized straight away, and a photograph and description of Anatole – who was already well known anyway – were sent to every military post in the country. But in the meantime, another lie was needed for when the princess arrived at her palace and didn't find her horse.

'They went the wrong way, Your Highness,' she was told, 'but they will be here in no time.'

The old lady went red with rage and blue with worry, and the brown patches on her hands turned white enough to make the whole Earth tremble. Fortunately, however, there was the Internet. Without that marvellous invention, it would never have been possible to find a suitable horse in time.

Anatole's twin was called Frison. Apart from a few hairs over his nostrils, which were painted grey by some professional makeup artists, Frison was the exact double of the princess's horse.

At the airport, where the cabin had remained, the dead Anatole was swiftly replaced by the new Anatole, the cabin was loaded onto a lorry, and at long last off it went to the palace. When the princess saw the lorry arrive with the cabin, she almost fainted with relief. She quickly recovered, however, and hastened to join her darling Anatole in his cabin.

The customs officials, the officers of the Red Guard, all in full uniform, and everyone else who had taken part in the hunt for the new Anatole stood there, waiting in suspense to see what would happen.

From the cabin came a howl of anger and despair. A few seconds later, the princess emerged, her eyes bulging.

'What have you done with my Anatole?'

'But… but… Your Highness – it *is* Anatole! Look – the same legs, the same ears, the same marks in all the same places…'

'It's not Anatole. It's not *my* Anatole. Anatole died three days ago. I want to bury him here, in my palace. What have you done with him?'

And so the Red Guard was mobilized again to go and find the remains of the real Anatole. Then for her dearly departed, the princess held a funeral that was both grand and at the same time very private. Anatole was buried in the middle of the palace gardens, in the shade of the biggest of all the aptly named flame trees.

Only after forty days of mourning did the princess bring herself to look at Frison, the unlucky lookalike. She went up to him, touched him, and spoke to him.

And wonder of wonders, she liked him.

My Uncles in America

★

Dear Uncles,

I'd like to ask a little favour of you. I want you to ring Mum, and invite me to America.

It'll soon be the Christmas holidays here in France, and I can't go skiing, I can't go to Disneyland Paris, I can't do anything. She is so furious with me because of my last school report that she won't even give me anything nice to eat. Just spinach and grated carrot, because they're supposed to make you clever. I got zero in practically every subject. Except two out of twenty for art. We had to draw views of our bedroom, and I drew a donkey. As it was a good drawing of a donkey, the teacher gave me two instead of zero.

She'll say she hasn't got enough money to pay for the trip, but I have an idea. You can tell her that you'll buy the air ticket for me. Between five of you, that shouldn't be too much of a problem.

She'll say that I'm being punished because I'm stupid. But I have an idea about that too. You can tell her I'll learn a lot on the trip. I'm sure that'll get her interested.

If she still won't agree, and if you really feel there's absolutely nothing else you can do, talk to her about Dad. Tell her that since he died, you've been thinking a lot about me, because I look like him, and you'd be upset if you couldn't see me. Something like that would work.

And that, dear uncles, is the favour I want to ask you.

Love,
Pierre

P.S. Don't forget the time difference – you don't want to wake Mum up in the middle of the night.

Dear Mum,

When I arrived in America, at my uncles' ranch, on the first day I couldn't understand a word they were saying, and I didn't even know who they were anyway. Bud, Bill, Brad – they all have names beginning with B, so I kept getting them mixed up. But in the evening, they gave me a hat and boots, and got me to ride Double Dream, Dad's horse. I was a bit scared, but all the same I went round the ranch, trotting first and then galloping. When they saw me coming back, standing in the stirrups and waving my hat like a champion, they all had tears in their eyes.

In the end, I decided to live with Bobby, who's married to Mary. I thought their daughter Dorothy looked a bit dim at first, but when I've persuaded her to cut off her plaits, she'll be great.

Dorothy's never fallen in love with a boy before. I must say, it's all very isolated here. At school too the kids are way behind. It's very small, the school. I've been to see it. There are about twenty pupils, no more than that, and they're all different ages, so there's no point in giving grades or positions in class. To be honest, I really like the American school system. The French system's no good for me.

Uncle Ben isn't married. He's gay. His partner Barney is gay too, and that's why they get on well and are always together.

The uncles talk a lot about Dad. Your dad did this, your dad did that, they tell me. And they teach me to do the same things. Like imitating bird calls, and finding wild mushrooms. Apparently I'm pretty talented, but maybe they're just saying that to make me feel good. I think they'd like me to stay here in America, and I'd really like to stay too. I could marry Dorothy.

Tell me what you think.

In the meantime, lots of love,

Pierre

P.S. I forgot to tell you that if you like you can come over here as well. There's a horse for you. Dolomite, a lovely mustang with a black mane, and no one's ever ridden him. You'd get on well with him, I'm sure, because he's highly strung – just the way you like your horses. Bud looks after him. Bud is the youngest of the uncles, and he's not married. It would be cool if you married Bud. But of course you'd have to fall in love with him first.

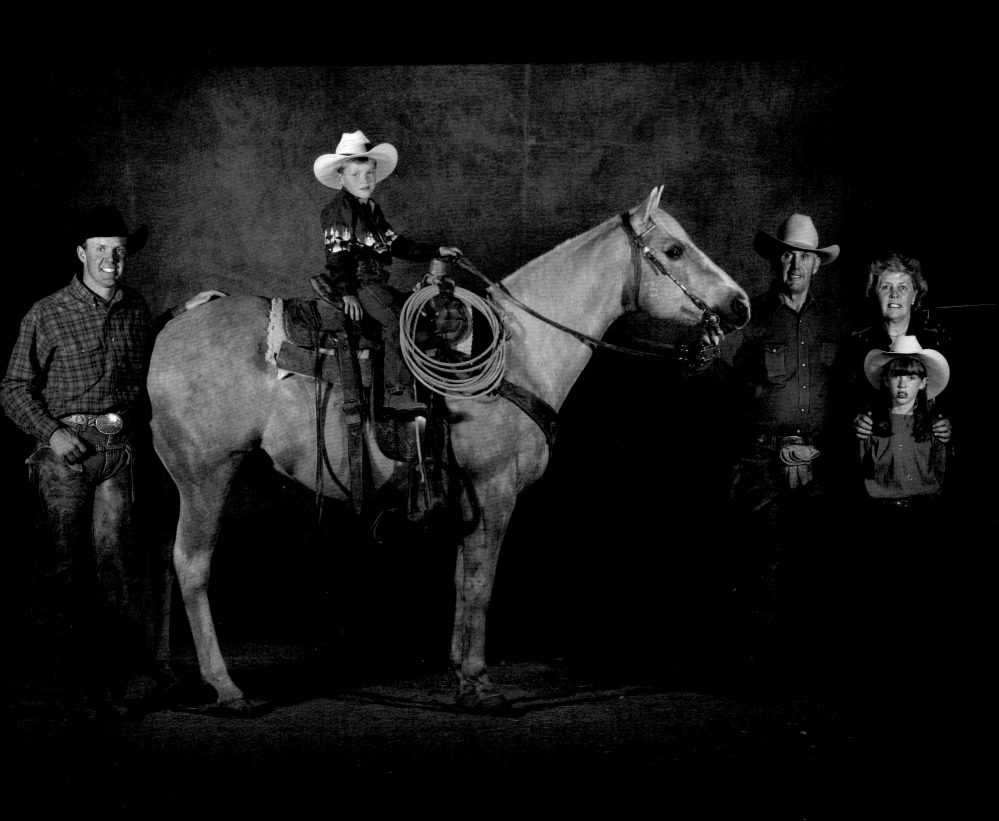

A Desert Rescue

*

My plane had crashed right in the middle of the desert. When I saw the wreckage of my machine, it didn't take me long to realize that there was no way I could repair it. My leg and shoulder hurt, and there was one question in particular that kept tormenting me: how had I managed to get out of this crash alive? Was I really going to survive, or was I going to collapse in a moment or two from internal bleeding?

Everything had died now – the plane, the wind, the sand, the sun. I sat down on a lump of metal and waited for Death to take me away. Then Ziad touched my shoulder.

'وقعت من اسماء ؟' (Have you fallen out of the sky?)

I turned round, and saw them all standing behind Ziad: his father Abdallah, his mother Hasna, his brother Hani, and his two sisters Zeina and little Amira, who came up to me, and felt my forehead with her hand.

'أنت ملك ؟' (Are you an angel?)

Before I could shake my head or wave my hand, Zeina was there too, holding out a gourd of water.

'أنت نسر ؟' (Are you an eagle?)

The water was so cool and fresh!

'هل أنت جندي ؟' (Are you a soldier?)

This was Hasna, their mother, speaking from behind her veil.

'A soldier? That's a question you never have time for if you're talking to a soldier,' said their father in English.

He signalled to his elder son, young Hani, who then came forward holding his horse by the halter. The horse was called Himish (The Spirited One), and was the family's prize possession – their treasure, their pride and joy.

It was also a great honour for them to give him to me, so that I could leave them and return to my own home.

Horses always bring out the best in people.

The Most Beautiful Horse in the World

★

By the light that shone from his skin, you would have said he'd been made by a goldsmith. And by the lines and curves and tensions of his muscles, he could have come from the dreams of a classical sculptor. That was Akhal.

The Queen of Slov had come upon this magnificent beast during a diplomatic visit to the mountains of Tambi.

'He's mine,' she said. 'I want him at home when I get back. You will put this gorgeous creature in the courtyard of my palace.'

'Your Majesty, it will be very difficult to capture Akhal,' groaned the Minister of Pleasure.

'But you will do it,' said the Queen.

She resumed her mission to the mountains. The Queen was having a great deal of trouble with the Tambi tribe, who for hundreds of years had been harassing the Slovian empire, looting the farms and burning the harvests, all for no particular reason. She had decided to sign a peace treaty with their chiefs or alternatively wage merciless war on them and finish off these savages once and for all.

The Minister of War was all in favour of war and of planting the Slovian flag on top of the highest mountain. The Minister of Finance was all in favour of peace, because he wanted to do business with the Tambi, buying their animal skins, wool and cheese, while he would sell them cameras, video games and mobile telephones, of which the Tambi tribe was sadly and totally deprived.

The Queen had to weigh up all the pros and cons, but in fact her mind was on other things. She couldn't wait to get back to her palace where, she thought, the most beautiful horse in the world would be waiting for her.

Men had dreamed for years of capturing Akhal. Some had taken the risk, but after a while all of them had given up. They would set out with their lassos, and their taming and training techniques, they would spend a few days waiting, watching, approaching,

Akhal could have come from the **dreams** of a classical sculptor.

using every possible and conceivable trick, even violence – but they always came back empty-handed.

The most beautiful horse in the world was impossible to catch. He glided between the air and the grass like a goldfish between pondweeds. You waited for him here, and he would turn up there, always with that look of haughty disdain, almost of mockery.

Lord Diensti, the Queen's Minister of Pleasure, was a wise old man. The Queen had left him a small troop of young soldiers to accomplish the mission, including some of the best riders, but he did not set out straight away in pursuit of the fabulous horse.

'Let us first think about it,' he said, walking along the line of military tents, his head bent and his hands behind his back. How could they capture Akhal when generations of trainers, horse dealers, hunters and riders had had to give up? Why could this horse not be tamed like all the rest? What sort of unquenchable, savage fire burned within this creature? Did Akhal consider himself superior, perhaps? Was he aware of his own beauty?

The master tactician used his binoculars to observe the great horse, to watch how he moved his head, always bending his neck to create the most graceful, most impressive curves.

'He is the reincarnation of Narcissus!' exclaimed Lord Diensti. Narcissus was a very handsome youth who spent his time looking at his own image in the water. He was so charmed, so overwhelmed by his own beauty that one day he changed into a flower – the very same one that still bears his name today.

At daybreak, the fires between the tents went out, and as the first rays of the sun broke through, it was revealed to Lord Diensti exactly what he had to do.

He melted down the swords and armour of his young soldiers, and with these he constructed a metal screen three metres high and five metres wide, which was carefully covered in glass by the blacksmith, so that in the end it became a huge mirror.

He had the mirror fixed to the back of several chariots, which were then pulled by ten horses to the river where Akhal normally went to drink. The troop of soldiers waited there without moving, without speaking, hidden behind the mirror.

Eventually, the most beautiful horse in the world arrived.

When he saw the mirror, at first Akhal thought it was an animal of his own kind, but it gave off no scent, and it uttered no sound. Of course it moved, and it shone, but it did not seem to have a life of its own.

Akhal went towards the mirror, and the horse inside it seemed to grow larger, reflecting each of his movements identically. Akhal then realized that he was looking at himself. How beautiful he was! It was unbelievable, these golden reflections, the supple lines and curves of his whole body. He was fascinated.

Akhal came even closer, his eyes fixed on his own image, so obsessed and so overwhelmed by his own beauty that he did not even notice that the mirror had moved. As he advanced, so the mirror retreated. Of course, Lord Diensti was controlling everything from behind the mirror. And so it was that slowly but surely, the strange convoy finally reached the palace. The Minister of the Interior ordered the gates to be opened at once.

What's happened to the most beautiful horse in the world?

They had no trouble leading Akhal, still glued to the mirror, into the palace courtyard. Then they unhooked the mirror and leaned it against the back wall of the court. All that remained was to wait for the return of the Queen.

After the Minister of Pleasure had been publicly congratulated on his skill, the people of Slov came flocking to see Akhal, while painters and sculptors set to work capturing his beauty on canvas and in stone.

What was the Queen doing all this time? She was negotiating with the Tambi chiefs, day after day after day.

Meanwhile, Akhal had put on every possible expression in front of the mirror. He knew exactly how to stand, and in exactly what light, in order to see himself at his most beautiful.

As the days went by, he was seen to be practising some kind of exercises before the glass. At first it was funny, but eventually one of the painters called out, 'Stop acting the fool!' Then everyone realized that Akhal was no longer the magnificent, majestic animal he had been before. His contortions and his grimaces were all an attempt to recapture the beauty that he was now gradually beginning to lose.

He himself became so miserable about it that he lost his appetite. He no longer felt like eating all the freshly cut grass that was brought to him every day. His skin became duller. The gold gave way to a rusty brown, like mud. And he stood motionless as he looked at the calamity reflected back at him by the mirror. He was just a shadow of the horse he had once been.

The Queen of Slov returned to the palace after three long weeks of talks, having finally signed a peace treaty with the Tambi. When she saw the horse in the courtyard of her palace, she sent for the Minister of Pleasure.

'What is that worn-out donkey that you've caught for me? What's happened to the most beautiful horse in the world?'

'He is there, Your Majesty. That is Akhal, but his beauty remained on the banks of the river and on the surface of the water, which holds all the beauties of the world.'

They set Akhal free, and from that day on he spent his whole life searching for what he had lost.

The Three Tenors

In those days, radio was still a long way off, and television was even further. If you wanted to hear opera, you had to go to the opera house. This did not stop opera singers from becoming famous, and of all the singers the most admired were, of course, the tenors. They could reach notes that nobody else could reach, and these would bring the house down. The greatest composers of the time wrote arias specially suited to their superhuman voices, to please a public that was eager for musical sensations.

People wondered just how high the famous tenors could go without bursting a blood vessel. If a tenor's voice cracked in the middle of an aria, he was finished, and like a bull at the end of a bullfight, he would be carried out on a stretcher and never seen again on stage.

At the time, there were three tenors who were greater than all the others: Giuseppe Sordino, Antoine de Gueulard, and John Breakglass. All three wanted to be known as the greatest tenor of all time.

In order to decide which of them was indeed the greatest, the Opera House in Milan organized a concert in which the three of them could compete with one another. It was a big event, because there had never been such a fabulous combination of singers, and tickets sold like hot cakes.

They started with some arias by Fusilli, an excellent composer of the period, though on this occasion the music wasn't important; all that mattered was the notes, and which of the tenors could reach the highest and hold them the longest. The whole thing was ear-shattering. But the public loved it, and they clapped and cheered and threw just as many flowers to one as they did to the others, so that it was impossible to decide between the three. The verdict, therefore, was a tie, and the three tenors went to the front of the stage, holding hands like the best of friends. But as soon as they'd gone backstage, they sang a different tune.

'Ah, you screech owls,' said Sordino to his rivals, 'I've never heard such rotten singing!'

'Singing?' said Gueulard. 'You call that singing? Ugh, not in my book.'

'I thought I was in the middle of a flock of geese,' said Breakglass. 'Aaaark! Aaaark! Even my horse sings better than you.'

'Your horse?'

'Have you got a horse that sings too?'

'I certainly have!'

'Well, well, well, that makes three of us!'

And so it was that a new contest was organized for the following day, between the horses of the three greatest tenors of the time. It was agreed that they should sing an aria by Paccani, notorious for its extreme difficulty. Once again the public were invited to choose the best, as signified by their applause.

That evening, Barnum's Circus gave a performance in the main square of the city, and there wasn't a single spectator. The churches, cafés and even the theatres were also empty. Everyone had gone to the opera to attend this unique contest.

'Singing horses? Imagine that!'

'And Paccani as well!'

'Impossible.'

'Ridiculous.'

'Scandalous.'

'They're taking us for a ride,' said the old music lovers.

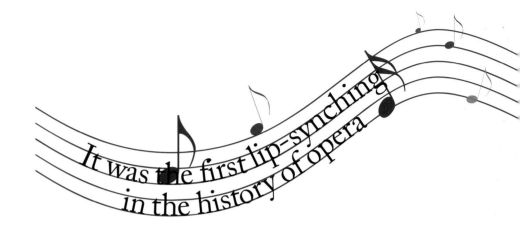

It was the first lip-synching in the history of opera

But they couldn't wait to see it, let alone hear it. Paccani himself was among the crowd, incognito, with a smile on his face. He was going to be the first composer in history to have his music sung by horses. He was positively whinnying with pride.

The horses were led on stage, and the concert began. The three tenors had, of course, been lying. Their animals couldn't sing. Each of their owners thought he'd been remarkably clever, however, because he'd hidden in the saddlebag a piece of machinery that most people didn't even know existed: a phonograph. The tenors had recorded themselves singing Paccani's famous aria, and so on stage all that the horses had to do was open their mouths. It was the first lip-synching in the history of opera.

The spectators were dumbfounded. Singing horses! Some women fainted, others went crazy, and a few

churchmen fell to their knees in prayer, uncertain whether this was a miracle or witchcraft. However, after the first moments of disbelief, the audience was won over, but once again the loud applause made it impossible to say which of the horses was the winner.

The tenors decided to take their show on a world tour, with each of them singing this and that in concert halls full to bursting. But things had now changed. The public were so keen to see the singing horses that the idea of going to see classical opera with real human singers didn't interest them any more.

And so wherever they went, the tenors had to go on stage with their horses. They attracted huge crowds, but the singers themselves felt humiliated by the triumph of the animals. You see, they couldn't tell anyone that it was them singing and not the horses. They'd been trapped by their own lies.

Thus it was that gradually the three tenors decided to retire from the stage. Giuseppe Sordino became a phonograph salesman, and John Breakglass devoted himself to the invention of a machine that was later to become a modest success: the clapometer. And as for Antoine Gueulard, he finished up as a horse-trainer.

Augustine's Obsession

✺

 'Augustine! You have the most beautiful hair in the world,' her mother used to say.

Women never missed a chance to run their fingers through her hair. 'How soft it is,' they would say, 'and how silky it is.'

'How beautiful it is,' said the men.

Augustine took great care of her hair. In the morning and in the evening, she would comb it for ages in front of her dressing-table, which was a fancy one with three mirrors that allowed her to see her hair from both sides and from the back.

As she became more and more vain, Augustine devoted more and more time to her tresses. It took her two hours every morning to style them. She had to get up at crack of dawn in order to get to school on time. And right up until the last minute, she would be correcting this tiny twirl and that tiny curl. Her mother had to shout up the stairs to make her finally tear herself away from the mirror.

The most extraordinary thing is that the secret of this style consisted in making it appear a total mess: there were spikes going in all directions, knots, curls, and strands which had to flop over her face in a careless fashion. The final masterpiece had to be doused in several coats of hairspray, because it had to stay in place all day long.

Augustine always arrived at school three seconds before the doors closed – you could set your watch by her, and she was always the last to enter the classroom.

At the age of eighteen, she almost failed her exams for the sake of an out-of-place roller, and it was only by a miracle that she passed the entrance test for business college, having had to redo her hair three times before leaving home.

At university, the preoccupation became an obsession. She now devoted three or even four hours a day to her hair. When she went to the lecture hall with her new style, some people showed their envy with giggles or whistles, others applauded, and a few fell in love.

It has to be said that Augustine varied her style according to fashion and the seasons, always opting for the most sophisticated, the most improbable and the most impractical variations. She never went to the hairdresser's, but did everything herself at home in front of the mirror, one strand at a time.

On the eve of her first day at work, her mother gave her a little talk.

'Make sure you do your very best,' she said.

'Don't worry, Mum, I intend to surprise everyone.'

With streaks and curls and tresses here, and braids and highlights and frizzes there, Augustine built up a hairstyle the like of which you've never seen before.

In the morning, the alarm clock rang, though it felt as if she hadn't had a wink of sleep all night. It was time for her to get up and do her very best.

Her head felt strangely heavy.

When she rubbed her eyes, her face didn't feel like her face. And when she touched her hair, it didn't feel like her hair. She leapt out of bed and rushed to the mirror. She almost fell over, so heavy was her head. And when she sat down in front of the mirror on her dressing-table, Augustine saw that on her shoulders was the head of a horse.

She didn't feel any fear, or panic, or even the tiniest pang of disgust. It was a magnificent horse's head, covered in soft black hair, with a pale-coloured mane of great beauty. A bit on the wild side. And then, when she shook this marvellous mop, she discovered that she could create an endless variety of possible styles.

Oh, how beautiful they were, the patterns, shapes and reflections. She shook her horse's head and laughed with pleasure. This was the culmination of all her work. Some people will say, of course, that she was just dreaming, and that's not impossible, but as far as I know, Augustine is still running around the fields, having at last achieved the perfect hairstyle: a mane.

Three Little Words

★

Phoebe's story

His name was Thomas. And he never stopped looking at me. But I pretended not to notice. In class, as I sat in the front row, I could feel him looking at me. He often put up his hand to answer the teacher, and when I heard his voice behind me, I trembled all over. He had a wonderful voice. A warm voice – a voice from the South. He must have come from somewhere exotic, I thought. I just longed for him to talk to me, just to me, with that wonderful voice. Instead, I sought comfort with Woolly, my pony, and stroked him for hours.

Thomas had magnificent black hair, and when it grew long, it seemed almost blue. There was no other boy like him.

When the teacher gave us our first monthly report, I was top of the class, and Thomas was seventh. But the following month, he'd gone up to fourth, and just before Christmas he was second. I wondered if he'd done it deliberately just to be near me. But I didn't dare believe that. Unfortunately, he didn't show the slightest interest in me. He preferred to be with his pony – a Dartmoor pony, black of course.

Because of that, I thought of dressing in black. I'd almost decided to do so when one day, I don't know why, he came and talked to me.

'Your name's Phoebe, isn't it?'

'Yes.'

That was it. Silence. It's all very well waiting for Prince Charming to talk to you, but if he does come along and you don't know what to say to him, you're not going to get very far. Anyway, he asked me why Phoebe was spelled with a Ph and not an F, but I didn't know. Luckily, he didn't know why his name had an H in it but wasn't pronounced TH-omas.

'It's funny,' he said. 'We've got weird first names, both of us. And we don't even know why some of the letters are there.'

50

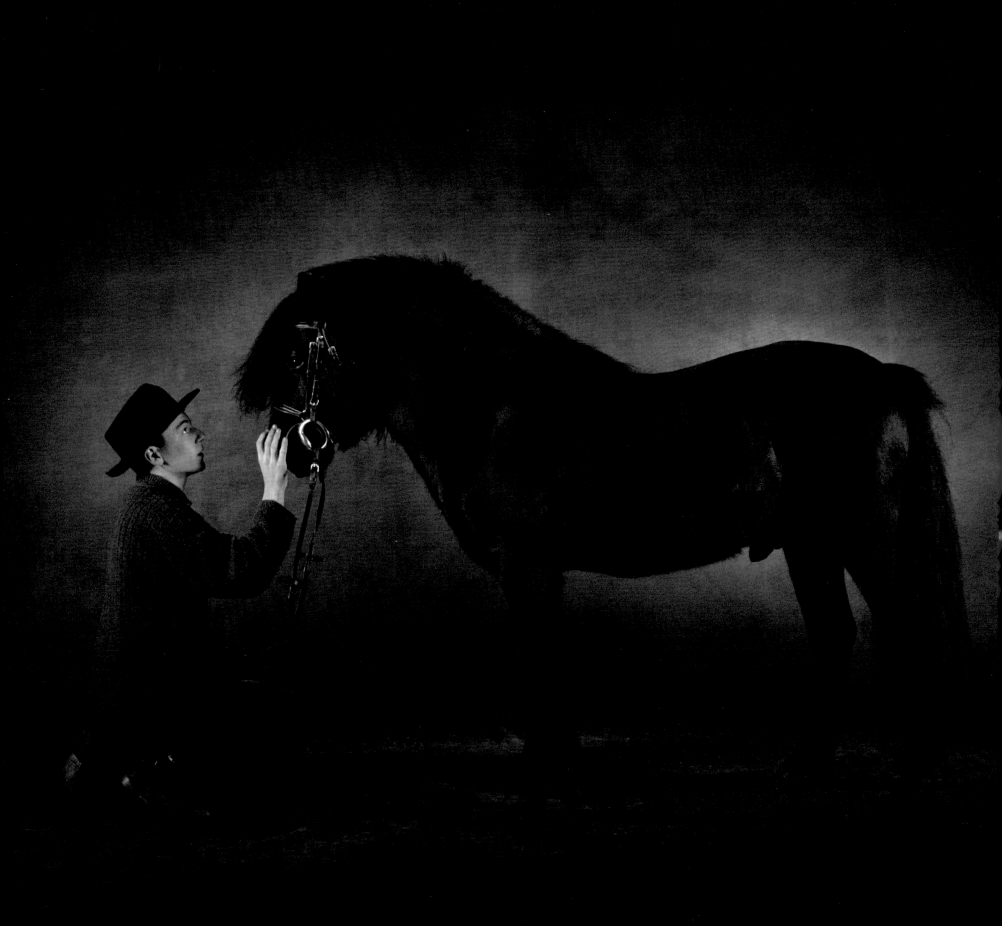

Thomas's story

I didn't dare look at her, she was so blonde. I didn't dare, but I did all the same, and I was transfixed. Her name was Phoebe. I didn't dare to say her name either, so I just whispered it to Zephyr, my pony.

'Phoebe,' I said, and shivers went up and down my spine.

In class, Phoebe was top in every subject. She lived in a very big house with a huge garden. Her father was a vet, and he'd given her a pony for Christmas. She adored it. It came to meet her at school, and she would pet and stroke it. It seemed such a sweet pony – a little brown Shetland, and super-intelligent. The sort of creature that can do absolutely anything except talk.

It was when I saw him that I decided to let my hair grow long, like the pony's. In the evening I dyed it secretly with peroxide, and I really studied hard so that I'd be second in class.

One day, I don't know why, I took the plunge and talked to her.

'Your name's Phoebe, isn't it?'

'Yes.'

It's all very well going up to a girl and talking to her, but you need to have something to say. Like an idiot, I hadn't prepared anything.

'Why do you spell Phoebe with a Ph and not with an F?'

'You do ask some funny questions.'

'So you don't know, then?'

'No. Do you know why there's an H in Thomas?'

She knew my name! I couldn't believe it!

Phoebe's story

I realized that he'd just said the first thing that came into his head. Because he was shy. But something had gone right through into my heart. 'Both of us.' That meant him and me. I started to say those words over and over again to myself.

Both of us. They were sweet and warm, those three words – as sweet and warm as my pony's coat, but the sweetness and warmth of the words were on the inside.

The Curse of Devil's Mountain

Hubert knew that the Upalatchis had hidden their treasure high on the peak of Devil's Mountain just before they had fled. It had happened three hundred years ago, but the memory had always remained fresh in Salmonrojo, because the Upalatchis had been such bloodthirsty rulers before the Kalamnos had come to liberate us.

The treasure of the Upalatchis, the fruits of so many years of pillage, was something nobody wanted even to touch. It was a treasure with a curse on it. All those who in the past had ventured to climb the peak had left behind their limbs, their heads or their sanity. But how much gold there must be in that inaccessible hoard! How many precious stones waiting on the summit of that accursed place!

Hubert, like most of the men in Salmonrojo, used to dream about the treasure. One day, as he was riding along the edge of the precipice, he suddenly found the solution: Springer, his magnificent horse. Springer was an exceptional jumper – the best there had ever

been in Salmonrojo. But would even he be able to jump that distance?

Hubert measured how far Springer could jump: 12.5 metres. But the gap between the sides of the precipice that led to the peak of Devil's Mountain measured 13 metres. Springer would land fifty centimetres short. But what is fifty centimetres to a horse that can already jump 12.5 metres? A little bit of training should do it, said Hubert to himself.

Every morning for a whole year, Hubert and Springer trained secretly at the riding school. What mattered most was that the people of Salmonrojo should not suspect what they were up to. When eventually Hubert would reach the other side of the precipice and find the treasure, he would leave this dry and miserable place for ever. He would go and live in France, near the Eiffel Tower, or somewhere like that. And he would live a life of luxury. The best restaurants, the prettiest women, promenading along the Seine. He couldn't wait!

Springer made all the progress that could have been expected of him. In six months, he was able to jump further than the 13 metres needed. Together they won several competitions hands down, and Hubert became well-known in the field of show-jumping. Everyone said he was an exceptional rider. They even talked of entering him and Springer for the Olympic Games.

13.10 metres, 13.20 metres…but to make absolutely sure, Hubert went on training him for another six months. And finally, Springer could jump just under 14 metres. Getting to the peak of Devil's Mountain would be easy.

'It'll be a piece of cake,' said Hubert.

One night, when the moon was full, he saddled his horse, whispered a few encouraging words in its ear, and the two of them went racing towards the precipice.

It was an amazing jump. It was a shame there were no spectators watching. It was as if Springer had understood the importance of the occasion, and had put all his strength into this one leap. He landed on the other side of the gulf without so much as a stumble. Hubert embraced his horse's neck, with tears in his eyes.

Then he started searching for the treasure. It was there, in the entrance to a cave. The Upalatchis had not even had time to bury it before they had fled. There were silver bracelets, gold cups encrusted with

Everyone started asking what had happened to Hubert.

diamonds, buckles, jewels of all kinds, dishes, silks, and huge piles of precious stones and metals. In all, it weighed more than 50 kilos. Hubert filled two bags that he had brought with him, and then he mounted Springer for the return journey.

'It's the high life for us!' he whispered into the ear of his four-legged companion. 'So now it's up to you. Let's go!'

He dug his heels lightly into the flanks of the horse, but it didn't move. Another dig, a little harder, and then a third, harder still. Nothing. Springer refused to budge. He had suddenly become as stubborn as a mule. And then Hubert realized why: his horse would never manage to jump the 13-metre precipice carrying 50 kilos of treasure on its back. This was something that he simply hadn't thought of.

Now Hubert had a choice: he could send Springer back to Salmonrojo with the treasure; sooner or later people would find it, realize what had happened, and send the horse back to fetch him. But once he went home, Hubert would certainly be given a hard time. 'So, you little crook, you were trying to get the Upalatchis' treasure all for yourself, eh, without telling us?', people would say.

The other solution would be to go back to Salmonrojo with Springer but without the treasure. He would save his own skin, but he would also waste a whole year of work and would have to give up all his dreams of a life of luxury. It was incredibly frustrating. Hubert, who was not the cleverest of men anyway, and always had to weigh up the pros and cons for ages before he did anything, took the bags off the horse's back, started pacing up and down, studying the sky, studying his feet, and knocking his head to punish himself for having been so stupid.

It was now daybreak. Exhausted and dejected, Hubert sat on a rock, his faithful horse beside him.

But after a while, Springer got fed up with waiting. There was not a blade of grass on this mountain peak for him to eat, and not a drop of water for him to drink. He took one more look at his master, and hey up, with one magnificent leap he sailed across the precipice and landed on the other side.

Springer trotted along through Salmonrojo until he was caught by Hubert's stable boy. Then everyone started asking what had happened to Hubert, and they looked everywhere for him – except, of course, up on the mountain, where he actually was.

They searched for days and weeks, and even ten years later the people of Salmonrojo were still wondering what could have happened to Hubert.

Journalists wrote all kinds of stories, and novelists invented all kinds of tales – including this one, which is as convincing as any.

CAPTIONS

◀◀ **Page 2 and page 63**
Guerrouan, an Arab Barb born in Morocco in 1995, palomino (pale mane and tail).

Page 4 and page 7 ▶▶
Ayacucho Coscorron, an Argentine criollo, handled by his trainer, Martin Hardoy.

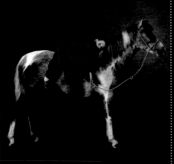

◀ **Page 9**
An Argentine Petiso pony, *Martin Fierro Mancho*, ridden by Ferdinand.

Pages 12–13 ▶
Kahela de Luc, a five-year-old French trotter mare. She is pulling a sulky, a light, two-wheeled vehicle used in trot racing.

Page 17 and page 19 ▶▶
Gylling, an Icelandic mare, ridden by Tota and then by Tota and her son. The high-stepping pace of this horse is known as the 'tölt'; it is very comfortable for the rider and is unique to the Icelandic horse.

Pages 22–23 ▸
Barb and Arab Barb horses.
Captain Djiby Tine is holding
Tango, ridden by Warrant Officer
Abdoulaye N'Diène, from the
military band of the Senegalese
Red Guard.

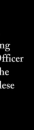

▲ Page 20
Daylami, a grey English
Thoroughbred stallion,
born in 1994.

Page 27 ▸
The cowboys of the La Cense
Montana ranch with their
Quarter Horses.

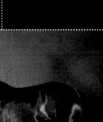

Page 29 ▸
Strip, a Quarter Horse, posing
with the Griffith family.

◂ Pages 30–31
Montana's GC Tracer, Missouri
Fox-Trotter, posing with Tymbre.

Page 33 ▸
Al Adeed Al Shaqab, a pure-bred
Arab, with the Al Qadi family.

**Page 35, page 36
and page 39 ▸▸▸**
Murgi, an Akhal-Teke stallion
born in 2000 on the Chamborant
Stud Farm, Russia.

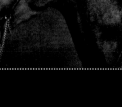

CAPTIONS

Page 42 ▸
Momino, a three-year-old Percheron stallion, presented by Michel Lepoivre.

◂ Page 43
Igloo, a spirited six-year-old Auxois stallion, owned by the Cluny National Stud and presented by Thierry Gallet.

◂ Page 45
Zorro, 13-year-old Maremmana stallion, shown with his owner.

Page 49 ▸
Felous, a nine-year-old rustic horse (probably Comtois) that has been trained to perform.

Page 51 ▸
Idole du Tregor, a twelve-year-old 'French' Shetland brood mare, with Pamela Mengy.

◂ Page 52
Epson de Kergroix, a ten-year-old Dartmoor stallion, with Fabien Bordet.

◂ Page 55
Koala d'Ivraie, a five-year-old Anglo-Arab stallion, ridden by Gilles Marnay, in the school at the Haras du Pin stud farm (Normandy).

Pages 56–57 ▸
Hortus de Pierre, a nine-year-old French saddle horse belonging to the Haras du Pin stud farm.

Translated from the French by David H. Wilson

First published in the United Kingdom in 2006 by
Thames & Hudson Ltd, 181A High Holborn, London WC1V 7QX

www.thamesandhudson.com

Original title: *Le plus beau cheval du monde*
written by Christophe Donner
photographs by Yann Arthus-Bertrand
published by Editions du Chêne – Hachette Livre 2005

Original edition © 2005 Editions du Chêne - Hachette Livre, Paris
This edition © 2006 Thames & Hudson Ltd, London

British Library Cataloguing-in-Publication Data
A catalogue record for this book is available from the British Library

ISBN-13: 978-0-500-54328-3

ISBN-10: 0-500-54328-3

Printed and bound in Singapore

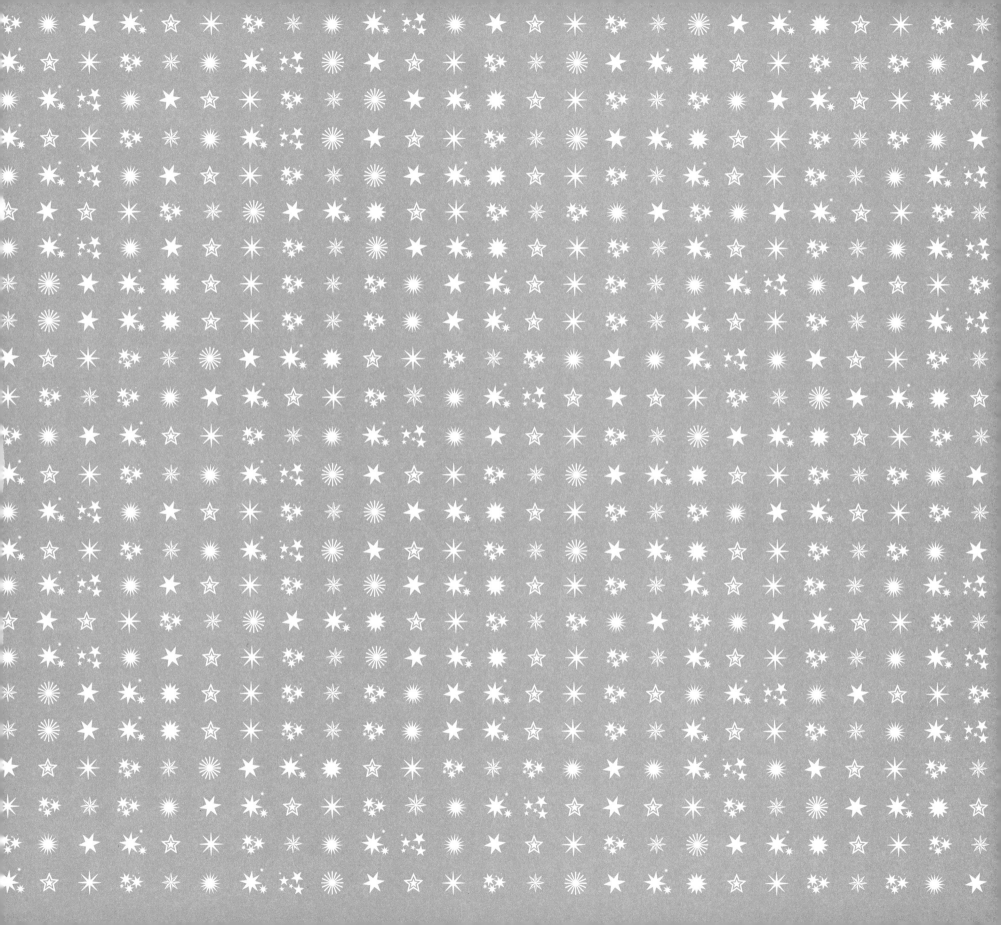

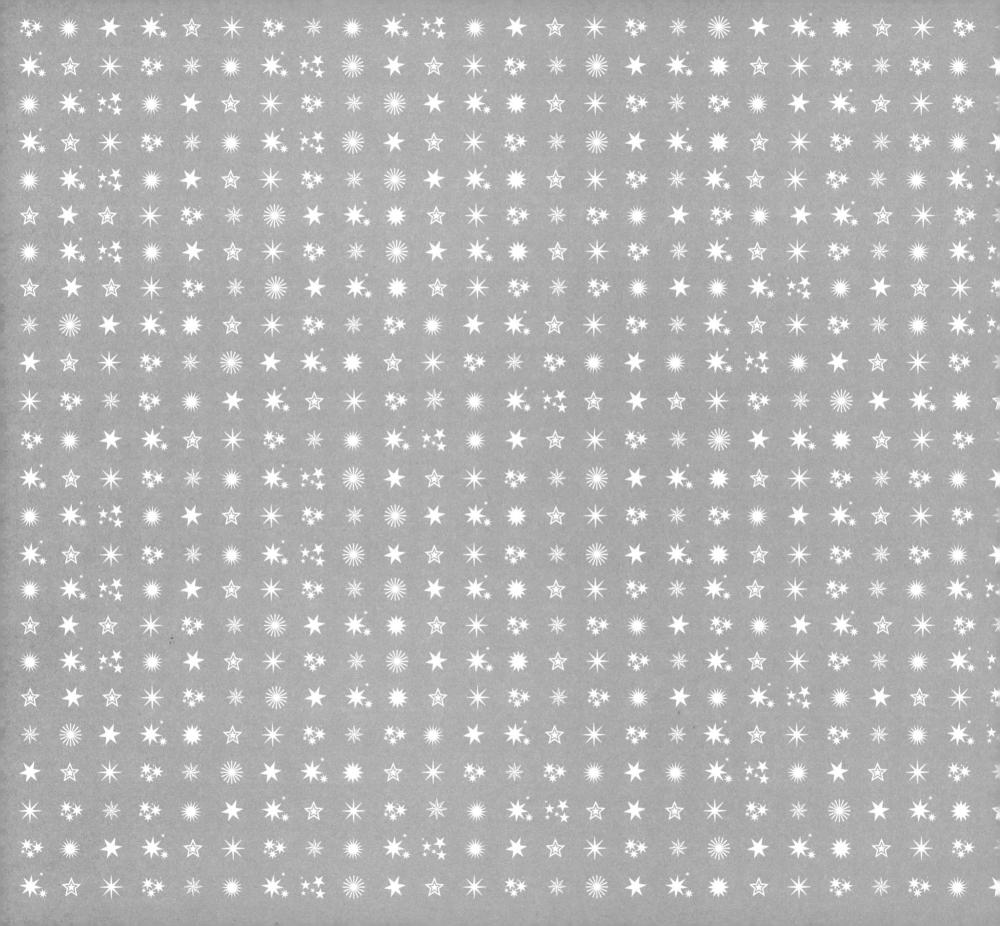